THE
HEROIN
GAME

THE
HEROIN
GAME

Bevelyn Hart

Library of Congress Control Number:		2021904610
ISBN:	Hardcover	978-1-6641-6234-1
	Softcover	978-1-6641-6233-4
	eBook	978-1-6641-6232-7

Print information available on the last page.

Rev. date: 03/15/2021

To order additional copies of this book, contact:
Xlibris
844-714-8691
www.Xlibris.com
Orders@Xlibris.com
824587

CONTENTS

Thirty-three people will compete in the game but only one will survive

INTRODUCTION

Why was this book written? Sometimes in life, there are just things you're compelled to do. Who did I write it for? For addicts and parents of addicts (PoAs) and those who love an addict. I realized that my story is the story of all loving parents who have been swept into the maelstrom of their children's addiction and that the bewilderment and torture that comes with it is shared by many. My story is every parent's story. And it needs to be told. I believe there are thousands (maybe millions?) of other parents out there who need to see that what is in their own heads and hearts is shared by others.

There is an important caveat to this tale; that this is *my* story, *my* experience at having a child who is a drug addict, *my* take on how an addict behaves, how they should be treated, what will and won't work, and most importantly, the impact it has on the friends and family members who love the victim. So there is no "right" or "wrong" to my beliefs, only my opinion as I see it and feel it. Maybe it's a "take" on the problem whose time has come. I'm not a doctor or a therapist, just a concerned mother watching my son's misery as he tries to deal with the situation and the system that helped to create it.

Many may scoff at my perceived ignorance, my lack of insight, my intelligence. But I stand by what I say. No layperson, no matter their level of intellect, can spend fourteen years witnessing the depths of addiction without having some worthwhile insight to its causes and characteristics.

These are mine. And if they're mine, then they may also be the experience of thousands of others who may not have been able to put their feelings into written words.

I'm sure there will be many a physician, therapist, and "authority" who will shake their head in disgust or frustration at this take on addiction. That's okay. I can only speak for what I have personally experienced. This doesn't mean that I know more than the "experts"; it's just that some things go beyond technical and intellectual understanding. Being the parent of a drug addict is like that.

Facts speak for themselves. I've been brutally honest about my experience, what I did "wrong," what I did "right," and where things stand today.

I will attempt to convey the pain a parent feels. We've all seen movies and documentaries showing torture victims. We all know about the Holocaust, medieval prisons, and the like. When you are a loving parent, you see the darling innocent baby you held in your arms, not an addict. Now imagine that baby being snatched from your arms, tied down, and being tortured. You watch while someone pulls out your child's fingernails, burns it with a torch, and your child is screaming in agony. You have two choices in this matter: One, you can stay there and watch. Two, you can vacate the room and pretend to go on with your own life. *Those are the only two choices. But you can't stop it.* Let me say it again. *You can't stop it.* I made both choices off and on in the last fourteen years. Talk about having no good options. It is the most exquisite kind of pain that I would never wish on anyone. In fact, I believe it changes who you are, much as some survivors of war experience.

Watching your child die from drug abuse is no different a feeling than a parent experiences with any sick child. Terminal cancer or the ravages of substance abuse, the parental pain is the same. In each situation, the source of the terminal illness is not relevant to the pain a parent feels.

I have never blogged or journaled or read studies or joined discussion groups on addiction treatment. Not that I don't advocate it, just emphasizing that this is what I've personally experienced, both directly with my addicted son and in society in general. This is not a synopsis of various opinions of others. For better or worse, it's completely my story.

Here's my experience with the "education" process.

I started as a virgin—that's how unknowledgeable and naive I was about the drug world. Not that I'm an angel; I just lived a very sheltered life in a very strict, old-school household and in a time when drugs were not as mainstream as they are today. I only used drugs twice, trying a passed joint in college. I'd heard of cocaine and LSD and mushrooms and other substances, but I'd never seen nor would I ever think of trying them. Today I am still a drug virgin. Am I polishing my halo? No, just trying to illustrate how blind I was to drugs. Should I have read up on the subject when my kids were teenagers? Yes. But I thought, *never my little darlings!*

I am sad to say now that I have a master's degree in the use and resulting behavior in the abuse of drugs. It's an education that I would have been happy to have avoided. Wish I could say it's a story with a happy ending. Maybe one day it will be.

It's important before we begin to define and clarify the terms often used throughout.

The statistic of the "3 percent cure rate" is used for expediency only and may be thought by many to be incorrect. Different studies show a permanent recovery rate from addiction anywhere between 2 and 4 percent. Indeed, it's possible to find studies that show a slightly higher or lower rate. For purposes of explanation and expediency, I have chosen to use the 3 percent figure and trust that it is accurate enough to defend the dialogue.

With regard to the term *"cure"* by this I mean an addict who has stopped using and remains clean for the remainder of their life. They are still considered addicts, even when recovered, but I use the word *cured* to define the condition. This does not include those that are clean for a time then return to drugs. The 3 percent refers to those who stop and never go back to drugs in their lifetime. My son's sponsor is sixty-five years old and has been clean for the past thirty years. He still goes to meetings every week. Is he "cured"? Only time will tell if he stays that way until his life is over.

To the doctors, addicts, therapists, owners of drug treatment centers, drug companies and their CEOs, politicians, concerned society, *please work together to change these grim statistics so there is a hope for the future of society.*

Finally, I often use the term *PoA* as a reference to "parents of addicts." It's important to note that it is sometimes a sibling or other close loving relative who goes through this experience with the addict, bearing all the pain and stress that comes with it.

HISTORY

Just like sports, heroin (and opiates in all their forms) has always been around. In ancient Greece, the Olympics came to be in 776 BC. Modern-day Olympics came to be in 1896. And the heroin games became a nationwide sport in the 1990s. Though opiates were around for centuries before that, its long-reaching effect on today's society really began following the cocaine craze of the 1980s.

Before mass production, promotion, and distribution of opiates (OxyContin, oxycodone, hydrocodone, et al.), street addicts hid in dark places on the outskirts of society, shooting up smuggled heroin. The media depicted them as down-and-out losers without a redeeming quality. Heroin was always around, but not in the hands of every curious high school student. Then in the 1990s, prescribing opiates became the thing to do. Why?

Promoted by drug manufacturers? Prescribed by doctors who believed what the drug companies and FDA purported about the benefits and safety in the use of these "miracle" painkillers? I could write a reference list of articles several pages long detailing progression of drug promotion, kickbacks, influence, and other factors, all of which created the perfect storm to addict a nation. Suffice it to say, that is what happened.

Within a few years, anyone in America with a hangnail could get a prescription. Unfortunately, the youth of America were quick to pick up on the high to be obtained by taking the pills recreationally. But let's not just blame it on the youth; thousands of people of all ages became addicted to the high.

My first experience with this phenomenon was by a nephew popping oxycodone for a knee injury suffered while skiing. Somehow, the "treatment" continued for months. About the same time, my twenty-six-year-old niece began having back pain. Enter hydrocodone. My son and his best friend from childhood didn't feign pain; they just bought the pills on the street when they found out what all the fun was about.

These were all young people in their twenties with high school and college under their belts and promising, lucrative careers.

I have no doubt that the above scenarios played out all over big-city

America, but surely not in the little towns of rural America. Hah! Kill that myth. Upon visiting friends in a small town (with a population of 2,200) in upstate Michigan, I learned that the rate of opiate abuse and addiction was out of control.

By 2000, it was possible to purchase pills on the street in every city or town in American. By the early 2000s, it was every addict's heyday; they were running from urgent care clinics to family doctors to quacks, to obtain prescriptions to fill at any pharmacy, relatively cheaply.

I even drove my son to a couple of appointments and pharmacies after he convinced me he was filling prescriptions for antidepressants. They were legitimate prescriptions as far as I could see. Understand that I was a neophyte in the whole understanding of the epidemic, as was most of America. One day I took my son to an urgent care clinic (La Costa, California). While he was in the doctor's office, I noticed in his backpack three empty bottles of the same medication from other doctors, which I indignantly took into her office. The doctor was busy writing him a prescription when I displayed the empty bottles to her. She sheepishly told him not to come there again but, believe it or not, handed the prescription to him.

This is how I discovered that something very wrong was going on.

In the first decade of the new century, this practice proliferated nationwide. Doctors' offices specializing in "pain management" sprung up like mushrooms in every city and town. There is much evidence that pharmaceutical companies were producing and shipping enough pills to some pharmacies to treat every man, woman, and child in the city. In fact, some areas received quantities exceeding their populations. There is no need to cite articles and news programs. The evidence to this is overwhelming in the media.

Finally, the federal government began to listen to the people instead of the drug lobbyists. A problem existed requiring diligence. A data bank was established, tracking individuals, doctors, prescriptions, and pharmacies. No longer could someone get away with what my son had.

Drug companies were put under scrutiny. It became harder to obtain the drugs "legitimately." By then, getting a legitimate prescription for opiates became difficult (ID required, no refills, no phone prescriptions, etc.). As is common with government, the legislation came too late, and when it did, it was overdone or applied differently by different doctors. One of my friends recently awaiting a hip replacement had to endure excruciating pain for two months because her doctor did not want to prescribe any pain medication. She had no history of drug abuse. Maybe his office had a prescription writing abuse problem? Maybe he was overly cautious? Who knows? So the very people these drugs are meant to help in an appropriate fashion were not getting access (Traverse City, Michigan). Concurrently in a different state (Palm Springs, California), I was hospitalized for emergency surgery, a noninvasive laparoscopic procedure. My doctor sent me home with a prescription for fifty hydrocodone. If I was going to need *that* much medication for pain, then he did something wrong. I used ten pills and threw the rest away. Why the disparity in writing prescriptions? Makes no sense.

Alas, the damage had already been done. The widespread and unnecessary distribution of opiates across the nation had already taken its toll. The "perfect storm" described herein created 1.7 million opiate addicts in the US as this is being written.

My son is one of them. Did someone put a gun to his head and force him to use? No. Let's just say that circumstances created an atmosphere and environment conducive to drug abuse. Combine that with a young man unhappy in his own skin, with unrelated mental issues, and voila! You've created the perfect storm for an addict.

By 2020, treatment centers had popped up like blackheads all over the country (more on that in later chapters).

When the prescription availability dried up around 2010, the addicts hit the streets. The underground market was flooded with pills, *but* they became expensive. Street heroin was a cheap alternative. Thus, the prescription opiate addicts switched to another form—heroin. Now all the control by the FDA was moot. Sorry, guys! Too little too late!

And so we come to the present day. Lawsuits being brought against the makers of opiate-based medication. More and more treatment clinics springing up. And more and more addicts than ever.

Should the drug companies be made to pay the cost of nationwide treatment centers? Sounds like a good idea to me.

Where will it go from here? Will opiates be outlawed? Doubtful. When prescribed appropriately, they are invaluable for pain control.

You see, the trouble with creating an opiate addict is that the "cure" rate is so low. I use the term *cure* loosely and will elaborate later. Heroin is one of the most addictive drugs known to man. Kind of a one-way street to hell.

My son is an addict. He started with oxycodone at the age of twenty-four in 2006. He's used fourteen years. I'm not sure it's even my son in there anymore or just the drugs talking.

Here is one mother's story.

Year One

He is an addict, newly formed and bewildered in the pleasure of the high and the pain of the withdrawal. He didn't even realize it when he picked up his game piece and took the first roll of the die. No one had read him the rules or explained the odds of winning or the paths that would be taken in play. Yes, there had been drug abuse warnings in school, but these were pills prescribed by doctors, not street drugs.

And I am a new PoA (parent of an addict), just learning the characteristics and ways of this new creature. Listing my observations is easy now. At the time, their presentation was insidious. He lived with a roommate, was a grown man, and I had a business to run. My agenda did not include "watch for signs of drug addiction in your son." What is common knowledge for me now was then strange behavior to me.

I believe it took several months for each of us to realize just what was happening. By the time we both did, it was too late. He was already addicted. He probably believed that it was a fun "party" phase of his life that he could easily move beyond. Fourteen years later, it still has him by the throat.

He had just leased a car; his business was doing well. All seemed right. Then he started staying up all night playing video games with his roommate. His place began to be trashier than his usual bachelor ways had been. Over the course of the next year, a pattern of traits and behaviors became apparent. This was the beginning of understanding that there was a big problem.

Since drug use is a deadly game with very few winners, let's start with the rules, which I can now clearly state for any potential players.

THE RULES OF THE GAME

1. Decide you want to play knowing that the odds of winning are 30 to 1.
2. Roll the dice. Begin by taking your first pill or smoke or injection. You'll know you are in the game when your friends and family start noticing the following characteristics:
     - Playing video games all night or spending all night with other "hobbies"
     - Staying out all night
     - Having erratic sleep patterns

- Paying bills late or not at all
- Much time spent picking pimples, sores, and scabs, resulting in scars all over the body
- Having the opiate "pig" habits—filthy room, car, body
- Missing work and/or losing job
- Losing weight
- The "head drop"—eyes closing and head dropping to the chest in the middle of a conversation, but only for a few seconds (addict is unaware of it and will deny doing it)
- Having withdrawals when you can't get it
- Sweating, nausea, flu-like symptoms, muscle spasms, and restlessness
- Hyperactivity
- Tinfoil balls in the trash, under the bed, in the bathroom—everywhere (sometimes it's little pieces of plastic wrap)
- Disassembled pens and cut-up straws lying around
- Extremely selfish behavior and narcissism to the point of doing harm to or neglecting loved ones
- Lying and sociopathic behavior uncharacteristic to your previous moral code
- Stealing
- Losing keys, wallet, passport, shoes, and/or various other items
- Manipulating tactics to borrow a vehicle or money
- Having a new group of friends
- Use of an inhaler (if a heroin smoker) or needle tracks (if a heroin injector)
3. Obtain money to roll the dice by any means possible. At first, you'll have money from your job. Once the job disappears, you will resort to the following:
    - Dealing drugs
    - Stealing
    - Selling possessions
    - Doing odd jobs far below your ability
    - Begging family members to help you
4. Draw a card and take action denoted on that card.
5. Keep playing until you are dead.
6. Anyone to finish wins. Everyone else loses.

DISCLAIMER TO PLAYERS OF THE GAME

If you are about to play the game, please know that this is a one-way street. The odds are 97 to 3 that you will lose. Three out of a hundred will find some way out of the maze to the winner's circle, but not unscathed by battle scars like rotten teeth, damaged lungs, and a diminished life span.

When you have played the game for a while, you will fully understand the odds of winning. The addict plays according to the rules (or by cheating), and no one else controls the outcome. No one can bribe the other players or pay to win.

Along the way, you will drag everyone you know or come in contact with into the game board, like a scavenger hunt they didn't want to play and will eventually quit when they realize they can't win and are only a pawn on your game board.

NOTE TO PLAYERS AND POAS

What makes up a person who wants to play the game? genes? upbringing? society? mental issues? a weak constitution? or simple boredom? *No one knows.*

That's why it's so important not to ever pick up a game piece, because no one knows who will be susceptible. Someone asked me once what I thought was my contribution to his addiction and/or what else in his life contributed to it. So much addiction philosophy promotes the following ingredients in the "recipe" for addiction:

- Family members with addiction problems
- Genes
- Household environment
- Child abuse
- Divorce of parents
- Psychological problems
- Poverty
- Upper-class "spoiled" environment
- Trauma in the family
- Trauma in war
- Trauma in relationships
- A death or loss

- Success or money
- Parents too lenient
- Parents too strict
- Sexual identity
- Self-esteem issues
- Low IQ
- High IQ
- Dyslexia
- ADD, ADHD
- Bipolar disorder
- Too short
- Too tall
- Too fat
- Too thin

I could go on but the point is made. All or nothing listed above can be a part of the recipe. The trouble is, no one has been able to draft the definitive recipe. While a case could be made for any of these conditions, or others not listed, how then do you explain the obvious fact that siblings raised in the same household can turn out completely differently? In the same house by the same parents. Same schools, same neighbors, same discipline. Same, same, same. None of my son's siblings are addicts, nor were they ever tempted to try drugs.

As to my influence on his addiction, or that of his father, I'm willing to accept culpability; however, I simply do not know what/if anything we did contributed to it. Because no one has the patented recipe, there is no way to distribute blame or cause. Is it fate or design? Perhaps when the knowledge of a drug's availability and use by peers and society in general occurs, the temperature is set to bake the perfect addict. I accept that all issues, from DNA to environment to parental influence, may be ingredients to one extent or another.

I believe somewhere in the human psyche, there is a recipe. We just haven't found it yet. And until we do, blaming anything or even attributing a set of conditions to addiction is futile. What purpose does it serve anyway? The benefit would be to recognize the set of circumstances before a child becomes an addict. In summary, *every* child should be watched.

The Heroin Game

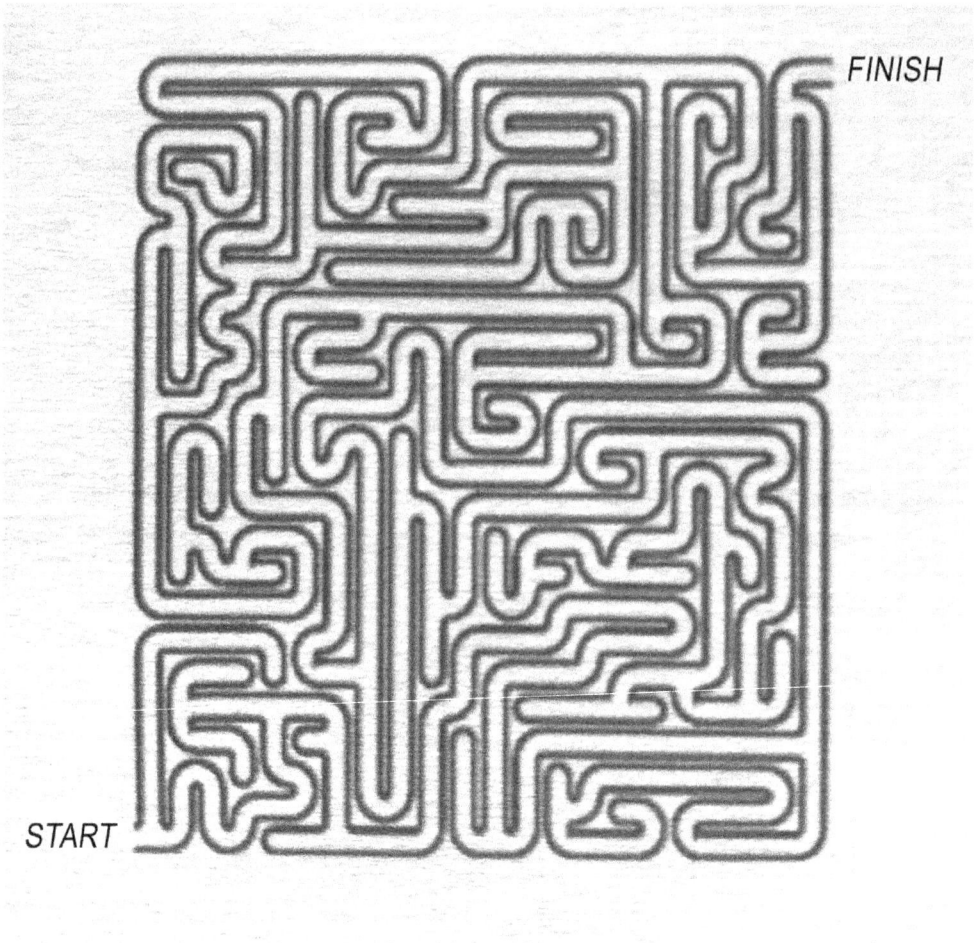

FINISH

START

GAME CARDS

Lost car keys. Go back one spot.

Arrested for DUI. Go to jail.

Stole some money. Celebrate with big party.

Rehab. Skip two turns.

Stole from sibling. Out on the street.

To hospital from overdose. Lose two turns.

To hospital from asthma. Lose one turn.

Overdosed. Go to graveyard. Game over.

Your wallet stolen. Go back five spaces.

Tooth fell out. Emergency visit to dentist.

Burglary to sustain habit. Go to jail.

Court-ordered rehab. Lose three turns.

Friend tired of you couch surfing. Out on the street.

Pneumonia from sleeping on the street. Emergency visit
to hospital.

Sores on face infected. Emergency visit to doctor.

Note: Addicts will be able to come up with many more game card options.

GAME TALLY SHEET

Number of Times

In hospital	_____
In jail	_____
Near death	_____
In federal prison	_____
In rehab	_____
On streets	_____
On a friend's couch	_____
On the run from debt collectors	_____
On your family's shit list	_____
In a sober living facility	_____

When addicts have played the game for a while, all will see that it's a game that can't be won because the addict makes the rules and no one else has control of the outcome.

My son has watched two friends die of overdoses, has been exposed to Mexican drug cartels, has defied a military lockdown curfew to buy drugs, and has been in the hospital numerous times. Nothing on any of the "game cards" ever led him to find the way to the winner's circle.

Anyone want to play? Or just throw in the cards and call it a day.

Year Two

He is learning the rules of the game, the "tricks of the trade" as it were. He experiences his first bad withdrawal, but it doesn't persuade him to quit. Nights of sweating and vomiting, which I mistook for him having the flu. At this point, I was still figuring out why the changes in his behavior were occurring. Bear in mind that PoAs usually also have their own life to live. With its ups and downs, trials and tribulations, watching over your grown children is not the concern that it was when they were minors under your roof. Even if I had realized sooner, would it have mattered? Is there a point early in addiction when intervention steps can be taken and the addict's life can be saved?

His business slows down, and his car is in danger of being repossessed. He's lost weight and his girlfriend. His credit card was unpaid; thus, his credit rating is falling. He is swiftly becoming not a participating member of the business world and financially self-sufficient but a person dependent on society, family, and friends.

Gradually, I came to realize what was happening. Now that I saw what was causing the problem, I was only looking to put an end to this crap. Yes, at that time, I thought I could. I had not read the rules. I didn't know this game was a one-way street. I had the same attitude that a lot of family and friends of the addict have: knock it off and shape up and get your life back on track!

From that day to this, I have tried to understand the draw to this substance. I know how it works chemically but still don't understand the feeling. When used for pain, opiates negate the pain without the person feeling "high." When used in the absence of pain, the body reacts with a feeling of euphoria. When the euphoria-causing substance is removed, the body becomes ill.

My son says life is too depressing without it, and part of me is angered and disgusted, thinking how the rest of the world deals with pain and loss and disappointment with their own strength of intellect and character. Why can't he?

What does addiction feel like? What is it about heroin that is so delicious that a person would give up everything for it? I've often wondered but never enough to try it. What magic does it do to make one ruin their life? I've asked my son to try to describe how it makes him feel. He tells me that it just makes him feel "normal." Whatever that is after fourteen years of addiction. I don't know if there is any of my son left inside his body. After years of using, is it possible for there to even be a "normal" for the 3 percent of recovered addicts?

Whatever the pleasure, I am in awe of what addicts give up for the drug high. This is what my son exchanged as a trade-off to play the heroin game:

WHAT HE GOT

- Drugs
- Jail record
- Scars
- COPD and asthma
- False teeth
- Bad credit
- Unemployment
- Homelessness

WHAT HE GAVE UP

- Family
- A future family
- Friends
- Career
- Education
- Financial security
- Youth
- Health
- Peace of mind
- Self-esteem
- A home
- A car (many cars)
- A place in society
- Happiness
- Food
- Sobriety (back where he was before the game)

WHAT HE'S MISSED ALONG THE WAY

- Five weddings of his aunt, cousins, and sister
- Four funerals of friends and family
- Three births of nieces and nephews

- Twelve Christmases, Thanksgivings, and birthdays

Yes, it certainly must feel very good if you are able to replace all that with one thing. I do not believe the developing addict has a clear picture of what they are trading for the addiction. The disease develops insidiously. They are well into the game board maze before they even realize it.

My son only sacrificed all the wonderful things in his own life. There are other horror stories of addicts letting their children get sick or starve to death because they cared more about the drug high than their own children.

What about the natural highs, like a beautiful sunrise, kissing someone you love, and a million other things? Every day to most of us is a brilliant gift to be cherished and enjoyed. Do those go by the wayside too? Does using drugs negate the ability to enjoy the natural highs that life provides?

Someone else I asked said using is like the world being in black and white and suddenly it's Technicolor. Might be better to be blind. Another said that it created a feeling of being able to "conquer the world."

Let's not forget that there are long-term effects to long-term drug use. It changes who the person is. The chemical effects, even when the addict is clean, can last for months or years. Even if "cured," are they ever really the person they had been before the drugs? I don't think so, especially when used during the years the body and brain are forming. So they've sacrificed their own humanity, their own soul and brain for the temporary euphoria.

It certainly must be a powerfully good feeling. Can someone please explain it?

I believe the addiction trap is much more complex than the chemically created "high." We all feel an endorphin high from things that occur in our lives (weddings, childbirth, the last day of school) without becoming addicted to the need to feel it every day.

In year 2, I was feeling shame that my son "had a problem" and kept it from everyone. I was angry, disgusted, and determined to get him back on track. I read up on the different forms of opiates, from prescription drugs (which is what he was using) to smoking and injecting heroin. Once he admitted to me that he was using pills, he seemed anxious to explain to me the various forms in which they came and how they were used and that "doctors prescribe them."

I saw that his friendships shifted from the lifelong school buddies and friends he'd had for years to a new group of "friends" who seemed to have no permanent address. Four years later, one would die from a heroin overdose. Some started "couch surfing" at his house. Although his business had dwindled to almost nonexistent, he waxed poetic about his plans to expand it nationwide and be a millionaire. Note to all: drugs talking!

As his second year of addiction was coming to a close, we did not foresee that he was about to enter the dependent zone. With no work, no credit, and no income, he soon had no home and no car. I think he wanted off the game board then, but guess what? It was too late. The rules didn't allow leaving the game.

WHAT YOU CAN/SHOULD DO

A. Encourage, support, feed clothe, lead to treatment

B. Nothing

Answer: The correct answer is B. Nothing.

SURVIVAL TECHNIQUES AND ADVICE FOR THE POA (PARENTS OF ADDICTS)

Our politically correct world would like you to believe there is a happy ending. In truth, there simply isn't. If there were a proven path to sobriety, it would be well-known, as is the treatment for diabetes (insulin) and the cure for bacterial infections (antibiotics). The fact is that there is no proven, or even semi-effective, method of treatment. If there was, the cure rate of 3 percent in 1999 would now be 10 or 20 or 90 percent. This has not happened. The best you can do is to cope and to make a survivable life for yourself.

Why do PoAs live such a sad life? Because they know in their hearts the truth. That doesn't mean that they won't always hope their child is one of the 3 percent. Hope for the 3 percent. That is my hope. That my son will have the miracle epiphany. That he will be one of the three out of one hundred and not the 97 percent dead or in prison.

Sometimes in life, there are no happy endings, just the sad facts.

WHAT ADDICTION DOES TO POAS

To say that his drug use changed my life is an understatement. It affected my relationships with men, with family, with friends, with neighbors, with business clients.

It changed the way I lived and wanted to live.

In business dealings, I actually let him work in my office, which ended up affecting service to my clients. This was done after he became unable to run his own business. I shouldn't have done it. It's the part of enabling that makes no difference to the outcome of the addict's habit or sobriety, but it affects the enabler big time. When sitting in board meetings, holding staff lunches, and navigating customer relations, I would always be wondering if his presence would affect my business and how much my employees knew. Again, it's that hope that giving them a "leg up" in the business world will help them become sober. Didn't work. My son is smart enough and has enough educational credentials to make a business success of himself *if* he gets clean. All I did was jeopardize relationships with my clients. I don't know if any of them figured out what he was all about, perhaps so if they recognized his situation because they were PoAs themselves. I found myself covering his tracks, and it added to the already stressful management position. This became a pattern over the next twelve years. His addiction piled stress on everything I was doing in my life. If this is a guide to dealing with being a PoA, then my advice is to discover sooner that you must draw a line between your life and goals and the addict. This is not because it prevents the addict from getting sober, as the "authorities" profess, but because of what it does to those who love the addict.

With regard to family relationships, much animosity was created. This is addressed in more depth in the "Blame Game" chapter. Everyone who loves the addict is affected, and there is a human tendency to start pointing fingers and casting blame where it is not due. Human nature, when people are disappointed or hurt, is to lash out at the nearest person, usually a PoA. This is why I kept many of the details of what was happening from other family members. Why bring them into the misery? Even if they are so inclined (as many are not), there is nothing that they can do, except lash out at others who are affected.

When it came to friendships, I was tight-lipped due to the inherent shame I experienced in the beginning. It's the idea of being classified in a group with the addict, that, again, he was a product of his upbringing, genes, etc. It took a long time to understand that I am no more responsible for his behavior than any parent is for the choices their offspring make. I no longer keep it under wraps, although my son feels ashamed and would like to keep it from everyone. It just doesn't work.

In my personal life, he affected my relationships directly by visiting his drug drama upon my boyfriends. Those who loved me loved him also. And by doing so, it put them in a place of being a surrogate PoA, with all the pain and toxicity that brings. By my seeing the writing on the wall and knowing what this man would have to endure if I married him, that he would be swept into the drama that has become my life, I couldn't bring myself to do that to justify my own selfish reasons. I've never remarried.

Then there was the toll of the sheer cost of time and money spent trying to stop the torture. Could my business have been more successful without this? Would my retirement nest egg be better? Could my personal life have been more fulfilling? Most assuredly. I think my son only began to understand his effect on others recently. He sees me lonely and troubled. Perhaps that is the beginning of the end of his addiction. Time will tell.

But the biggest effect it's had on my life is with my sense of well-being and peace. It's living life "waiting for the other shoe to drop." Waiting for the call that his body has been found. Waiting for a call from the county jail. Waiting for his plaintive voice on the phone saying he is freezing under a freeway bridge and hungry or that he can't breathe. If he had died of cancer (for example), I would be able to mourn his loss but go on to put my life back together and keep my happy memories. This is like an agony that won't end, perhaps for the rest of my life.

The learning process has been fourteen years long, and it's been the school of hard knocks, tears, and desperation.

Am I alone in this? Absolutely not. Perhaps there is a comfort to all of us to be able to clearly state the effects of addiction to the addict's loved ones.

When I went to an NA meeting the first time, I wanted to speak. My voice cracked, and when I opened my mouth to squeak out the words "My son is an addict," I could say no more through my sobs. The box of tissues was passed. I'm much better now. I can talk with clinical detachment of a sort.

At a Nar-Anon meeting (Carlsbad, California) a few months later, a mother a few years older than me rushed in late. She wanted to speak and was given the floor. She stated that she finally had a good night's sleep the night before because her son was arrested and in jail. At the time, I found this bizarre. I was a fairly new PoA, and my son had never been in jail. She further stated that she was able to sleep so well because, for the first time in months, she knew where he was that night and that he was safe. I was new to the game but have come to feel the same way she did. You see, it's the not knowing that is the killer of your soul.

My hair stylist explained her personal experience. It was her brother, not her child, but the love is the same. She said she realized one day that the brother she knew and loved wasn't in there anymore. His body was just an empty shell holding nothing human. The search for the drug was his only motivator, and lying or doing anything necessary to obtain it was okay. She says he's two years clean now, but not the same brother she grew up with. Forever changed. And so was she.

Dreams die hard in us human beings. We all have hopes and dreams for our children (president of the United States maybe!). Mine went from seeing him as a successor to the family business to being a real estate entrepreneur, to working for other entrepreneurs, to unemployed, to waiter, to handyman, to functioning in an institutional environment, to just being alive. Now that dream is dying too.

Why do PoAs live such a sad life? Because they know in their hearts the truth, that not enough is being done to help the addicts. Until and if that happens, it's a lifelong heartache and worry that can't be assuaged by any events, no matter how joyous, until there is a cure. That is my hope. That my son will have the miracle epiphany. That he will be one of the three out of one hundred. That he will win the Heroin Game.

Years Three, Four, And Five

He continues to play through the game board, relying on me, his siblings, his father, and his friends for financial support. He couch surfs, apartment shares with roommates, and lives with family. By this time, his credit is ruined and his health is deteriorating.

Hindsight is so clear, but at the time all this was unfolding, we continued on with our lives, considering his "problem" to be a temporary annoyance and embarrassment. Surely he would get over this "party" phase of his life. After all, he was only twenty-four when he started. He was probably feeling the same way.

As a couple of years passed, we alternated between stages of disbelief, of hope, of anger, and hoping our love would "cure" him. We tried intervention, counseling, medical doctors, rehab, etc., but he, at that point, was not even willing to admit that he had an addiction that he could not control. Nor did he want to stop, but he still believed he could any time he decided to.

This was when we began to impress upon him the cost to his financial well-being. He'd worked hard to be certified in his profession and worked hard to buy a new car and build a credit profile. The fact that he was throwing all this away, he either failed to recognize, he rationalized that the financial downfall was caused by "other" factors beyond his control, or more likely, he simply didn't care. One of the "great" side effects of opiate use is that it creates a euphoric sense of well-being that makes the user believe that all problems can easily be conquered.

As a warning and disclosure to addicts and PoAs, let's make the monetary ramifications of an addict's life abundantly clear. An addict living in the real world is no different than any other being, in that there is a cost to feeding, clothing, and sheltering. In addition, there is the cost of the drugs and the medical care that their use will engender. So let's address the financial aspects.

Just in case you're better with numbers than theories, here's some for you.

Cost of living: $40,000 annually (minimum in Southern California)

This is what it costs for an adult to be self-supporting (or supported by others). Some geographic areas could be more or less; this is an average, and that takes into consideration receiving state-funded medical care.

This is what drug addiction costs annually on average. Some use more; some use less.

$70.00 per day at an annual cost of $25,480

So on average, this person's existence on the planet (in the US) costs $65,480.00 annually *minimum*. That's without tickets, jail bailment, fines and loan sharks, doctors, dentists, and emergency room visits. If it seems I am being moronic to state something that should be self-evident, remember that the addict would like to sweep the cold, hard facts under the rug. They live from day to day, and sometimes hour to hour, so their cost on society is not an issue to them.

It's a good bet they are not paying this themselves. Guess who's paying? You, the taxpayers, and private donations, theft and illegal activities.

Because drug abuse has become a national disgrace, multiply the costs per addict. All these addicts need to eat and obtain drugs. A good percentage of incarcerated persons are there on drug-related theft and other crimes. Just an added bonus to the costs borne by taxpayers. Thanks, drug manufacturers.

So in his fourteen years of addiction, over $900,000 has been spent for his support and his drug habit. A small percentage of this money came from his own wages. The majority was provided by family, friends, the state, and charity.

Again, just a cold, hard reminder to *you* and to the *addict* that their chosen lifestyle is not without a monetary cost.

A note to addicts: If you're not funding your lifestyle, someone else is, be it the government, your relatives, or your friends. Just don't kid yourself about how expensive it is and whose paying for it.

You've seen in this chapter how unrealistic it is for an addict to fund his habit *and* put a roof over his own head and feed and clothe himself. So how do they pay for their habit?

TRICKS OF THE TRADE

Besides the obvious sources such as theft, drug dealing, and prostitution, you need to know the more subtle ways that a novice drug addict's parent may not be familiar with. This usually occurs in the first couple of years while you are still in the "help" mode and naive about their ways. That was the case for me, and I had to learn the hard way that I was supporting the habit without knowing it.

- Trading food stamps for cash or drugs
- Cashing in gift cards you thought were safe to give them because it's not cash (There are actually websites and apps that allow trading gift and debit cards for cash.)
- Pawning anything of value—electronics, instruments, appliances of their own (Later, they'll pawn your computers and jewelry if they can get their hands on it.)
- Cash from family and friends (Hint: it's *always* for drugs, not food or other "emergencies.")
- Government aid—welfare, medical disability, etc.
- If they have a car, using it to transport their dealer, with drugs as payment
- Getting "credit" from dealer (This gets very dangerous, especially when dealing with cartels.)

These are the few I personally encountered.

Then, of course, they resort to theft. They almost always start with stealing from people they know, *not* strangers. This seems ironic, but think about it. They assume friends and family are less likely to press charges and have them arrested. And they're right. It starts subtly—a twenty from the wallet, the use of a credit card. I had to resort to a safe for my purse, jewelry, and keys when he was around. This actually was one of the hardest adjustments and brought me the most shame. I was raised on honesty and morality, and so were my children. I grew up and raised my kids to be honest and trustworthy. My mother's purse sat on the table every day of my childhood, and I no more would have touched it than fly to the moon. Neither would one of my children when they were growing up. Addicts have no morality. You must remember that when you want to see the beautiful child you gave birth to. They become sociopaths, just a little side illness from the addiction. It becomes all about the drugs. The hunger transcends all other needs and moral considerations.

Before he got into drugs, he had my account PIN; that's how much I trusted him. Two years later, he used it to withdraw $2,800 over a period of four days. Should have changed the PIN. Hindsight. And the bank wouldn't let me prosecute because I gave him my PIN. Ditto when he and his girlfriend stole my SUV. Couldn't report it stolen because he had the keys, implying my consent.

Know the laws and protect your things if you ever suspect drug use. Don't learn by experiencing what I did.

Many addicts are a danger to society and specifically to their families—stealing from grandparents, holding their parents at gunpoint, traumatizing siblings, neglecting and abusing their children. An addict is more likely to do harm to those they know than the general population. Convenience? An attitude that they won't be prosecuted? Remember that when securing your house to keep out thieves.

They rarely steal drugs, however. Apparently, there's honor among addicts. Thereafter comes robbing strangers and drug dealing, hence the "go to jail" card.

THE BLAME GAME (AND HOW TO AVOID ITS TOXICITY)

Dealing with people around the addict can be very destructive for PoAs. In my experience, there are several "blame game" types categorized for expediency:

- The holier-than-thou, perfect parent
- The guilt-trip maker
- The comedian—making a joke of it
- The healer—Superman steps in to save the day
- The judge—guilty by association

Addiction affects so many more people and relationships than just the addict. I hope they can see that or care. The nature of addiction is narcissistic and sociopathic, so it probably doesn't occur to them or bother them.

My family, circle of friends, and group of business associates is very big. Eventually, almost all found out that something is "wrong" with my child. The ones who are easy to deal with are (a) those who have an addict in their own family and (b) those who don't give a darn, too busy with their own problems. The rest must be dealt with. The self-righteous ones are the worst because you're not human if you don't feel guilt on some level.

The majority of my friends and acquaintances didn't know the situation or maybe they did but didn't want to say anything, or maybe they thought I was too stupid to know what my son was and they didn't want to be the one to tell me. It's especially hard when you have family members who overtly and covertly blame you for the child's addiction or, at least, for not "curing" it.

One of my favorite behaviors is assigning me the "mouthpiece" for the addict by my family. They may be afraid of him or repulsed by him, or they want my take on his condition. Or it's a way of showing me I'm responsible for him. My family either says nothing at all about him for months or years *or* they begin asking me how he is—if he's using, if his in rehab. Yes, I'm his mother, but that does not make me his doctor, therapist, private secretary, or translator. He has a mouth and a phone. They all have his number, so why not call him? I already know the answer, and I don't like it.

They already know how he is—he's still an addict. Because if he went through full recovery, it would be shouted from the rooftops. What is really being asked is, (1) Are you enabling him? (2) Have you gotten him treatment yet? (3) Why haven't you cured him? There are many more "Why haven't yous" that have been asked, all implying that if I'd just get smart and get with it and care, he would be cured. It's all a "guilt trip" game. I would love to think they really care about him. But then wouldn't they call him instead of running their communication through me? They see it as *my* responsibility as his mother to fix him. So they walk away shaking their heads in disgust. One elderly relative is quite outspoken, asking why I haven't done this or that for him / to him and lecturing me about addiction—a subject about which she knows almost nothing. She is convinced he's just "being a lazy bum" and, if given enough tough love, will "pull up his bootstraps" and behave properly and get his life together. Wish it were so!

Then there's the healer, which is kin to the holier-than-thou person. Since you've utterly failed your child for years, they'll take the reins and step in to end the addiction. The person in my life who did this is an RN by profession, so she, of course, was an expert on how to treat him. She made me agree to cut all communication with him and stay out of his life, implying that I had clearly been the reason he was still an addict. This I did gladly, stepping back and wishing with all my heart she did have answers I hadn't found.

Well, two weeks later, when he'd failed to show up for rehab, taken money from her, and disappeared, it was clear she had no more answers than anyone else. The fact that she was disgusted and appalled that he failed to show up for rehab, borrowed money, and disappeared is what puzzled me. He was behaving exactly as an addict does. If she's an expert, why would she be surprised? She was not privy to everything I had done for fourteen years, so maybe she thought he'd never been to rehab. I just can't figure out what she thought she would be doing differently.

I am puzzled by all the "expert" advice offered by others who have no qualifications to do so. They often know less than I do yet speak with authority and conviction. The attitude is that they know what should be done and I'm the idiot who can't figure it out. I qualified all my opinions with the caveat that they are only mine and that I don't expect them to be shared by everyone, and I expect the same from others.

I hope that other PoAs do not have the same problem, but I suspect there are enough of us experiencing the blame game that it needs to be brought out in the open. I've dealt with it in the following ways:

- Said nothing, ignoring their inquiries
- Pulled out a slip of paper with his phone number on it and said, "Call him" (This is met with shock, bewilderment, or anger)
- Answered as honestly and succinctly as possible (The comments I received afterward made me wish I had taken choice number 1.)
- Said "I don't know how he is"
- Said "Yup, he's still a drug addict"
- Lied and said he's great

I'm braver and more honest now. I tell them it's not my job to report on him or watch him or be his mouthpiece, so they can call him if they really want to know.

No one has.

In defense of the "blame game" types, it may be all they are capable of in handling a tough/sensitive situation, much like what to say to someone when there is a death in the family. Not everyone knows the right thing to say/do. For that, they can be forgiven.

Something friends and family may not realize is how much pain PoAs are in. Every moment of our lives is colored by being the parent of an addict. A lot of things many people do without thinking—watching violent movies, news about child abuse, wars, sick children; celebrating holidays and birthdays; looking at childhood pictures—all can bring heartache. I mean really, folks, it's not easy to eat a Thanksgiving dinner or celebrate the holidays when your child is in the torture chamber. If I think of him hungry, it's hard to choke down a holiday feast. I must repeat to myself, "He created this situation. He is the only one who can change it." Life must go on, of course, but the heartache is always there.

My extended family seems to deal with his absence quite well. I think they are oblivious to how painful family get-togethers are for me. The stoic "out of sight, out of mind" philosophy? Are they jaded beyond emotions? Or do they simply not care, lacking empathy? No matter. It just puts a further alienation between us.

How do we handle all the pain and face the odds *while* we're working at our careers, raising other children, and trying to be happy and productive? If we are not always smiling, try to understand.

I have many close, loving, and well-meaning friends; they hurt when they see me hurting. So in the times over the last fourteen years, when I have let my son in my life, I've been lectured by them to stop. And I get it; they're only telling me what I already know. Most have offered unconditional love and support. The time line for a PoA to assimilate the emotions addiction engender and to figure out the proper course to take cannot be dictated by others. It's a personal journey of misery and disillusionment.

As with some friends, there has been similar behavior to that of family, talking to me like I can do something about his addiction, things like "Get him into rehab" or "Get him on methadone." Advising *me* implies that his life is in my control and is my responsibility—both untrue.

Some have tried humor, making a joke and making light of his addiction. One of my best friends has a seven-year-old little girl. I don't think he'd appreciate me making fun of her if she turns out to be an addict. Of course, he knows his "little angel" would never turn out like that! Here's what I'd like to say to him: "I am tired of your cavalier attitude about my son. I know you find his whole drug problem hilarious and like to make jokes about it. BTW, they're not funny, besides being distasteful and inappropriate. How would you like it if your beloved daughter grows up to be a hooker or drug addict?" 'Oh no! Not possible!' You say, 'My angel would never end up like that!' Whether she does or not, he wouldn't appreciate jokes about her.

I'll never get over the hurt about my son, and it's *not* a joke.

Which brings me to the self-righteousness of many whose children are stellar human beings. I am happy for them, but the holier-than-thou attitude is unnecessary.

And finally, the guilt by association. Because of his illness and banishment from family gatherings, relatives' homes, etc., I have, on occasion, also been banned. I have also been judged for his sins. Again, it goes back to the parent being held responsible for producing an addict. In some cultures, family and spouses are held accountable for another's sins. Apparently, this also occurs in modern-day America.

The one thing that was in short supply is genuine empathy/sympathy and an understanding of the pain and disappointment of the PoA. I guess it's just one of those things where you have to walk in someone's shoes.

So, friends and family, I'm here to tell you that not any of you, nor I, can be the answer to his problems. Attempting to counsel and advise the parent of an addict just creates a level of guilt that is undeserved.

Admonishing the PoA for actions they have taken or not taken just hurts and causes guilt. The PoA may not be far along enough in the process to accept that enabling serves no purpose except to cause further misery to the PoA.

If the person wants to talk, listen and offer love and not judgment. That's all you can do.

It's a long process from discovering your child is an addict to those around you finding out. It's an evolution from guilt to accepting blame, to the criticisms and comments of others, to finally accepting outside input for what it is—another person's opinion and reaction to something they are not personally experiencing. This is your own journey, and no matter where you are on the trail, it is not for others to tell you how to walk it.

Need I say that all the questioning cuts like a knife? Not only is it painful but also frustrating to realize how little they grasp the dynamics of the situation as I finally was able to do.

Even when you've come to terms that you are not responsible for the addiction, there are those with the following mindset:

- You are responsible for it.
- You could have prevented it.
- It's in your power to cure it, if only they can get your idiot brain to understand that your actions caused or contributed to the addiction.
- If only you'd been harder or stronger or nicer or weaker.
- It doesn't matter if your other kids are not addicts, you did something wrong with *this* one.

At the times I took him in, when he was trying to get clean, he became healthier from eating better and having a roof over his head. Did that exacerbate his use? No. Did it decrease his use? No. Did it appear to others that I supported his drug use? Perhaps. Did it delay his physical deterioration into dying of drug abuse? Probably. Was that a bad thing to delay the inevitable? Maybe. If enabling is so terrible, why don't addicts die because of it? My experience is that the healthiest my son ever looked was when I "enabled."

The joyful times are when the addict is in periods of sobriety, and most will have these. You ask yourself if this is the real thing or another false alarm. It's a period of false hope, followed by the heartbreak of dashed dreams when you find a fresh stash and realize they're using again. Their short-lived "clean" times don't make for a productive citizen. It only adds another layer of agony for the family when they relapse.

It's helpful during these times to remember the 3 percent. Almost all will have periods of sobriety. But 97 percent will continue the game.

PARENT'S MANTRA (REPEAT AS NEEDED)

I did not cause my child's addiction.

I have no power over the problem. My actions have not prohibited, perpetuated, exacerbated, mitigated, or cured the problem.

Enabling will not cure or kill my child.

Enabling will damage me emotionally and financially.

Years Six, Seven, And Eight

At this point, all hope of him having a viable career is gone. He cannot obtain credit, has no job, and has worn out his welcome with family and friends.

We discover he is buying his fix on the Mexican border south of San Diego. Now he is playing in the big leagues, and his life could be in danger. Although he's been using for half a dozen years, he is still naive in the ways of the third world. He considers these animals whom he is buying from his "buddies." That is what the drug will do. He does not understand that if he shorts them on one payment or asks for "credit" that he will be eliminated and probably tortured first. Again, it's that feeling of well-being engendered by the drug.

I don't know if living in San Diego naturally led him to the border, or the fact that I had a beach house fifteen minutes away was a draw. Now I live in fear of him showing up at my house and knowing that he could unwittingly draw me into his dangerous situation. At the end of year 8, this matter comes to a head with him realizing he could not continue to associate with the border rats, and he moves fifteen hundred miles away.

At this point, he had avoided jail, for which I was thankful. Still hoping he would be clean one day, I knew he would have a better chance of putting his life back together with no criminal record. I do not have the same concern today. Not only do I now understand the "three out of a hundred" factor, but I also hold diminishing hope that he will be one of the 3 percent.

All is not lost on me, and every year is a learning process. Lessons learned came not from NA or counseling but from observing his behavior and habits and observing the drug community surrounding him.

When he relocated to another state to live with his father, I hoped for the best, not realizing the state he went to had one of the biggest opiate abuse problems in the country. No matter. It was really everywhere, and I now know he would find it anywhere.

Out of sight, out of mind? I knew he was in the torture chamber, but I was not in there with him, watching. I knew without asking that he was not clean, because then I would surely be informed. Still, not having to watch the ravages of addiction on a frequent basis gave me some level of peace, or at least a break from the constant drama.

I've now come to realize that my lifetime of hard work to build a business success story has suffered financially in my effort to "help" him. My learning process has gone from disbelief to acceptance to a lifetime of heartache. I am also beginning to understand that the "help" I have given him has affected only me. It neither helped nor hurt him, but it drained me of my money and my soul.

As I learned later, I'm glad I did not have the kind of money that would have afforded a $30,000-plus-per-month treatment center. I've now learned that this "five star" treatment has not improved the 3 percent cure rate any more than the low-cost government-subsidized and charity-supported clinics. The rehab return rate exists for all levels of treatment. Again, the game allows for circling back into rehab for years, with the addict still never reaching the finish line. For a PoA with limited finances to fund such a process is futile. I've met several PoAs who have bankrupted themselves in the search for a cure.

After two years, he comes back to San Diego. He remains as addicted as ever. There was something of a wild animal about him. The once impeccably groomed businessman now looks like the homeless person he is. His skin is tanned from living outdoors, camouflaging some of the sores on his face. He is thin but with the leanness of a wildcat living on instinct. He walks with a toughness, a pseudo purpose to his wanderings. He no longer looks like the son I knew, but an alien creature.

Of his choice, he goes to a detox lockup facility and rehab where he was clean for a couple of months. He takes steps to update his career recertification on line. I'm hoping he will stay clean. He is confined to the house and has no access to a car or money, but it was not long before I see that he is not completing the online work and then "borrows" my car without my knowledge. It is difficult to put a person under twenty-four-hour lockup without sacrificing your own freedom.

We realize that he has again started buying drugs on the Mexican border from people who would as easily kill him and put his body in a vat of lye as sell him drugs. He was arrested by Mexican police for being in the drug district.

The learning process continues through these years. I've moved from rooky to student and am well on my way to a graduate degree. During the phases of addiction, another factor became evident.

This information will help PoAs understand the addict, but it is suggested that the addict be encouraged to read this information to gain a self-understanding.

Aside from being narcissistic with leanings to being sociopathic, most addicts are in denial about the impact their habit has on their lives and the lives of others. The rationalization technique they use usually involves the "poor me" play and blaming their bad luck on other people, other circumstances, and the universe in general. I've most often seen this situation take one of three forms.

The Unfair/Unfriendly Treatment

With my son, this ran the gamut between colleagues backing out of business deals to girlfriends dumping him. With all the anger he had and reasons he could come up with regarding their "unwarranted" behavior, never did the fact that he is a drug addict and that they may have known or discovered that, have any bearing on their actions. The elephant in the room was invisible to him.

The Manic Drive to Achieve Goals

My son was ambitious (with drug-induced mania) and would spend hours, days, weeks on a goal or project. Whether starting a new business enterprise, buying real estate, refitting a car, etc., he genuinely could not understand what was in the way of his goals. Hello. The elephant in the room. He would spend hours laying out his plans to me and asking for advice on where he might be going wrong, and my answer was always the same year after year: "You can accomplish anything you want to in this world. You're bright and ambitious enough and goal-driven. There's just one problem. Your addiction. With it, you will never accomplish anything. Without it, you can accomplish anything."

Unfortunately, it was always met with argument that

---

something else must be the problem. I never did get through to him.

Masters of Their Own Fate

Addicts tend to be masters of their own universe, and that works against them. The fact that this practice got them into exactly the predicament they are in, is not understood. To ask "how's your plant been working for you?" is futile. Never mind that it hasn't worked for them thus far. They do not want to relinquish control of their lives to another person or entity.

You see, he was convinced (probably like most drug addicts) that he could manage his addiction. That he could be a functioning drug addict. I've watched him do it over the years, thoroughly convinced that his job performance, relationships, and behavior would not be affected by the drug use. It never worked for him. Invariably he would lose clients or his job due to poor performance. Casual friends who were not drug users didn't want to be associated with him, and his close, lifelong friends lost tolerance for his erratic behavior. Only the fellow druggies stuck around. He argued many times that he could display "normal" behavior when high, but to others, the characteristics were blatantly obvious. To this day, he's convinced that he can be a functioning drug addict.

I think the ability to rationalize in this way is to avoid the decision to give up drugs. That's something their mind cannot accept. They think that surely there is a way to just use a little or just at certain times and still have a successful career, happy marriage, etc

The PoAs also play a version of the deny ability game. One part of it is not wanting to admit to or believe the low odds of their loved one recovering. These first eight years of his addiction, I took steps to keep him out of jail. I bailed him out and paid traffic fines. My thought was that if/when he recovered, he would have a good chance for success in the world without a crime record following him. By the time he reached his early thirties, and as I understood the low odds of him becoming clean, I no longer cared

---

34

about his record. That ship has sailed. Now his going to jail would be of no consequence, and I would not bail him out. Nor would it serve in his favor, as I've heard drugs are very easy to obtain behind bars. He might be sent to a mandatory rehab program also.

For the PoA, the gradual process from denying the odds of recovery to accepting those odds can take years. The advantage we have is not having our vision clouded by drugs, only by love and hope. I've come to see the situation in its truest form now. It doesn't make me happy, but at least I'm not in denial. It's easy now to not buy into his manic ideas, his belief that he can be a functioning addict, and his belief that he could quit any time he really wanted to.

Years Nine And Ten

He travels fifteen hundred miles away to his father's house, hopefully without repercussions from the drug dealers.

While he lives with his father, I am convinced he is using as much as ever and will not stop. His father dies, and he remains in his house until it is sold. Then he spends a winter in a tent under a freeway bridge in the snow at temperatures of seven degrees below zero.

He returns to San Diego hoping to live with me, but I won't allow it. He goes to rehab, then to a sober living house, where he is caught with drugs. His sponsor takes him under his wing, and he is watched 24/7. He is finally clean for three or four months and hates life.

IS THERE TREATMENT/HELP FOR THE ADDICT?

This is a babe-in-the-woods account of the steps I took. I felt completely alone in my quest, as my family doctor of twenty-five years could offer no help, nor did NA provide any resources. It was frustratingly hard to get any direction. The only eager parties were private facilities, and this was only because they were making a sales pitch. I've since learned a lot and mostly from addicts who have run the course themselves, having been forced to treatment by the courts.

What did I find help-wise? Pathetically little. I'll hit on a few points.

- Sober living facilities are privately run, very expensive, and notoriously full of drugs. They are supposedly regulated by the government but are mainly left to their own devices. The "landlords" of these facilities, whom I met, were only interested in collecting more rent on their broken-down houses than they could ever get from one legitimate tenant. One that my son went to was $600 per month to share a ten-foot-by-twelve-foot bedroom and shared bath in a rundown house. According to him, everyone was using something (Vista, California).
- State-run rehabs are overcrowded. Drug addicts don't handle a waiting list well. They need to go in the day they decide to do it because tomorrow they may change their mind. And they have to be willing, or treatment will fail, they say. A word to rehabs: since only 3 percent will find permanent sobriety, it's a revolving door. If the state can't afford that expense, let the drug companies pay! Facilities won't take the unwilling, unless it is court ordered.

- The only way to get into a state-run or charitable facility for longer than three weeks is to be ordered there by a judge in court as part of punishment for committing a crime.
- Private facilities funded by donations and government subsidies (one in San Diego) have waiting lists and require daily calls from the addict. Perhaps the process of making them call every day is to test their sincerity or to cull the number of patients to a manageable group. Drug addicts can hardly function, yet they are expected to have the presence of mind to follow a daily call schedule?
- State and charitable facilities do not address underlying mental issues, which there almost always are.
- Private facilities cost tens of thousands of dollars. Their success rate? No better than doing nothing.
- In the areas we lived, NA groups were surprisingly few and far between. My son claimed that these meetings were of no help to him. I also attended meetings for the families of addicts, but I couldn't participate without crying hysterically. I was a newbie to the addiction world at that time and might do better now.
- Many of the services we looked in required lengthy red tape and jumping through hoops on the part of the addict. I heard secondhand that this is so they can "prove" they're ready to get clean. Addicts can't even coordinate a bus ride or shower!

Was this futile search due to a lack of diligence on our part? Could I have pursued more relentlessly? Perhaps. But I must then ask the question, why should these services be so elusive that a PoA of average intelligence cannot navigate through? I took the steps a reasonable person would take in this situation, and it lead to nothing affordable or proven effective. Let's not forget that the addict is also expected to navigate through the system when he is sometimes barely able to survive daily life.

If affordable options and services were available at low/no cost, I was unable to find them. Nor was I informed of such by any of the medical/drug therapy people I encountered. Over the years, several people in my group of friends and family hinted that services were available but were unable to provide specifics. When I was given leads, they never panned out.

So what's the magic potion for recovery? Alas, no one knows. If rehabs are so effective, why do patients (addicts) keep going back again and again? The truth is, nothing has proven to be significantly effective despite all the research and declarations by "experts." If *any* treatment (and I mean that in the medical term and in behavioral term) were effective, it would be shouted from the rooftops.

I've personally heard a lot of different reasons from recovered addicts as to what triggered them to quit.

- Tired of the merry-go-round of being in and out of jail.
- Becoming a parent
- Death of a friend or family member
- Damaging their health to the point of being in a care facility
- Being gravely injured
- Tired of being homeless

But for all these answers, there are probably many, many more. It's such an individual thing that to label a process is presumptuous.

I even daydreamed about locking my son up in a secluded cabin hundreds of miles from civilization for a couple of years. Would he come out and go right back to it? I finally had a semblance of that scenario in reality when we were stranded on a Caribbean island, which was put under military lockdown when the COVID pandemic hit. Confined to our homes under threat of arrest and unable to leave the island, he *still* found a way to obtain heroin.

Maybe it's a gradual combination of any and all the above and simply getting older and believing in death and how short life is that makes an addict open to recovery. *But* never have I heard that it was from running out of drug money or being in rehab or friends or family ceasing to enable.

I defy someone to tell me how all the rehabs (big and small), all the doctors and therapists, all the hope and prayers of a nation have increased the permanent recovery rate of 3 percent. They will definitely have my attention, my gratitude, and my hope for my son.

So what *is* effective? No one's figured it out yet, and that's what all the experts don't want to put out there. It's too awful to say. Well, I'm saying it. If there was a significantly effective treatment plan, the "cure" rate statistics would bear that out. Yet the figure was 3 percent twenty years ago, 3 percent now.

Are we still in the experimental stage, or is the answer simply that there is no "cure"?

My personal hope is that the answer is somewhere in the total physical/psychological analysis of an addict, which no one heretofore was willing to pay.

Drug companies and quacks do so much damage to family and society; perhaps they should be locked up for life. For make no mistake, they are responsible for locking thousands of addicts in the torture chamber for life.

In the past, I felt guilty for not researching more, not trying harder to find the answers. I don't now. When I realized there are no answers—no magic cure—I stopped beating myself up. All the facilities, all the doctors, all the funding and medical treatments have not changed that 3 percent.

Many in the medical field are adamant that addicts should search out answer for themselves. They can't even take a bath, so how can they handle their own treatment? Nice idea, just not practical. People with mental illness who cannot function are admitted to psychiatric facilities, often against their will. Why are mentally and physically impaired drug addicts not treated the same way, for life, if necessary? We all know why. There wouldn't be enough space by half to accommodate them.

One of the times my son was eager to go into a treatment place, they said we didn't get there early enough. He'd just flown in from his father's house in another state. It was raining, and I was sick. I fell to my knees in tears at the outside door of the treatment center. I was broken and unable to cope. They said to bring him back the next day, so I kept him in a hotel room, staying up all night to make sure he didn't disappear.

This is only one experience of the times he's gone to treatment.

Now others may have had a very different experience or found it easier to get help and answers. I can only speak from my experience.

In conclusion, unless you are rich, court ordered, or a very functioning addict, long-term treatment is not available. That's my take.

Ironically, the area in which there was a lot of help was the pop up of quack (I'm being kind here) clinics where licensed medical doctors sold themselves out to the cause (Vista, California). With offices catering to addicts, a $100 visit (*cash only*) got you a five-minute exam and a prescription for Suboxone, Adderall, or Xanax.

I think that most homeless people on the streets of most cities are mentally ill with substance abuse problems. Our society does not take care of the mentally ill, obviously. Does the state have an obligation to take care of its misfits? A political question . . .

So it is up to the person himself (who is totally unqualified to do so) or the families of the person to seek help for them. Could I have him declared incompetent and get legal guardianship over his life? Don't know the feasibility. It's not easy to take away one's freedom in this country. He is not insane but still unable to run his own life. Then there's the unhappy fact that I would become legally and financially responsible for all his actions, and without locking him up twenty-four hours per day, I would not want to be in that position.

It is said that a society is judged by the way it takes care of its very young, very old, and infirm. We don't have a very good track record.

Do I sound bitter? I am. I'm frustrated that the conditions occurred to create this epidemic. I'm frustrated that the best minds—the experts in addiction—can't find a viable solution to the problem (even though they speak as though they have). And I'm frustrated at the addicts whose brains are so poisoned that they can't help themselves get to the end of the game as a winner.

It is my belief that most addicts have underlying mental health issues that are not treated, my son included. He has always been socially withdrawn and subject to bouts of depression. I don't think addiction can be treated without treating mental problems also. (Mortgage the house or win a visit to a talk show where the host offers to cover the cost!) This type of treatment is extremely expensive. It is my experience that no one from the county rehabs to the $300-an-hour psychiatrist address these issues. In fact, the worst of the bunch was the psychiatrist. She charged $170 for five minutes of her time—the time it took to write a prescription for Suboxone (Encinitas, California). So good luck with that, addict. It's hard enough to get treatment just for addiction or mental issues. But both? Hope you're a millionaire. That brings us to another contributor to the low rate of recovery. Addicts are usually having a hard time coping with life, obviously, or they wouldn't have resorted to self-medicating. So now the odds of them getting their life straightened out are even lower.

Drug treatments for drug addiction don't work. Suboxone never helped my son stay clean. It cost a fortune, however. There were mandatory visits to the psychiatrist every thirty days at $170 per visit. Prescriptions for Suboxone were over $100 per month. And all it did was help him avoid withdrawal symptoms when he ran out of heroin—and to better hide his heroin use, since he never showed signs of withdrawal. He was only on methadone for a short time; It was costing $400 per week on it and I was simply unaffordable. Plus, after each dose, he was high as a kite. I've heard it can be obtained at no cost now, and I told him that. Guess he hasn't been able to fit pursuing that into his busy schedule. Being a drug addict is a full-time job, and they're usually looking for help from an assistant.

Private clinics pretend they are the ultimate solution. I remember clearly the last call I made to a private drug treatment facility several years ago. The conversation went like this:

> Me: How much is your treatment plan?
>
> Addiction counselor: $30,000 per month
>
> Me: And where's a heroin addict supposed to get that kind of money? If he had that much money, he'd be spending it on drugs.
>
> Addiction counselor: Sometimes insurance covers it.
>
> Me: How many heroin addicts have health insurance or even a job?
>
> Addiction counselor: Well, families sometimes pay.

I hung up. There you have it. The older generation is expected to go bankrupt paying for these private treatment facilities, which have a negligible success rate and high recidivism rate.

As to the addict taking responsibility to find the help himself, investigating options is often beyond the capacity of someone on drugs. Yet many a drug treatment center proceeded with the attitude that addicts are fully functioning citizens.

MY THOUGHTS ON DRUG TESTING

Over the many years, I went through periods of time when I tested my son's urine. Sometimes it was clean, sometimes not. A couple of times, I caught him using a test-tampering device (google it!) so that the test would be negative. In the end, it became a "cat and mouse" game in which I lost interest.

The truth of it is, you'll *know* when they're clean, when the physical and behavioral evidence indicates.

The biggest indicator when they've been clean for a period of time is that they'll *shout it from the rooftops*. They'll name the date and time they last used and celebrate it. If they are not doing that, they are still using. Don't waste $29.95 on a home testing kit.

THE ULTIMATUM

Here's a good time to mention the "ultimatum" method of drug treatment. This is used by treatment centers and parents in their home. Basically, it says the addict can stay as long as they test clean. If not, they are out! This is supposed to cure the addict? I've never seen it work. This assumes the addict has a desire to please the party imposing the ultimatum or to avoid living on the street. The sad fact is that it doesn't work. It turns out to just be a side game played by those around the addict. They'll lose a little time, and your efforts will have been wasted—not to mention $30 for the test kit!

The 3 percent who recover will follow orders and meet expectations without ultimatums.

DEBUNKING POPULAR FALLACIES REGARDING RECOVERY

1. *Effective means of treatment have not been found.*

   If your child had cancer, you would spend everything you have to save them. But with a 97 percent failure expectation, would a doctor even suggest doing it? That's the failure rate for drug addiction.

Believe me, if a viable cure or even promising treatment has been found, it would be plastered in the headlines. It isn't. Yet all the public and private treatment facilities approach addicts *and their families* as though their systems work and are worth the money. If this were true, we'd be swarming to the wormhole, and addiction would be a thing of the past.

Parents like me would mortgage their house, max out their credit cards, and borrow to pay for that "cure" that would pull their child through the keyhole and out the other side.

As a matter of fact, we *do* spend that kind of money—on unproven cures and treatments in a desperate attempt to have our child back.

Everything I have known to date has varied efficacy. Not that society shouldn't try, just not at the expense of the addicts' loved ones and the public. *Drug companies should pay.*

Here are the addicts' possibilities:

1. Full recovery, being clean the remainder of their life
2. Functioning addict
3. Jail or prison
4. Rehab or treatment center
5. Homeless on streets
6. A rotation of 2–5
7. Death

At one time or another, the addict may repeat numbers 2–5. There's no repeat on number 7.

What is the secret to achieving number 1, being the top 3 percent? Alas, no one knows, and anyone pretending to is lying, because it's different for everyone in that 3 percent. The addicts and the few recovered addicts that I've talked to all have different answers.

2. *Preparing for the addict's death is not pessimistic; it's practical.*

So statistical reality is that you must prepare for your loved one's death. Does this sound harsh and pessimistic? Sorry, I'm just looking at the stats. It *is* harsh, but its reality.

Actually, during the times my son was on the streets in a rough part of town, homeless in subzero weather in Utah, it actually helped that I'd said my goodbyes. We'd shared all that we could together, I did lie awake at night sometimes crying until I couldn't breathe—my pillow soaked—at the thought of him cold and hungry. That's the torture part for the PoA - that you know what is happening but you're not watching. And lest you want to say "His choice, he can end his agony," know that there is something about stopping addiction we don't understand and never will.

Here are some suggestions on the reality of your loved one's death game and how to cope:

- Prepare mentally and emotionally for the death as best you can.
- Do not hold yourself responsible.
- Work hard to steer your life away from it.
- Abandon your current life if you must, to protect your sanity and (dare I suggest?) happiness.
- Make funeral arrangements and practical preparations as much as possible to make it easier when the time comes.
- Remember that if they are alive, they are in torture over going through choices 2–5.

I have a friend in my beach resort neighborhood in Mexico. She'd come from Texas. Her son has been an addict for years—in and out of jail, breaking into her house, and generally terrifying and invading her everyday life. She could no longer handle the emotional distress and fear, so she sold her home and everything she owned. She picked up and moved to Mexico, leaving no forwarding address. She has begun a new life and says she feels calm and at peace for the first time in years (Baja, California, Mexico). She doesn't know whether he is in jail, dead, recovered, or on another area of the game board. She decided to remove herself permanently from his torture chamber, and for that, she has some peace of mind. A little drastic perhaps, but she is free to start a new life. I'm considering taking this step myself.

Now some "experts" might say this is a ridiculously unnecessary measure to take. But when you are a single, older woman, no restraining order can protect you. Many people are killed by members of their own family who are addicts. Then there's your heart and soul; nothing can protect those.

3. *Media is misleading about the methods used to "cure" addicts.*

I have a pet peeve about watching TV talk shows dealing with addiction, many of which purport to know the methods to "cure" addiction or that there are good consequences of an addict hitting rock bottom, which they *will* and *successfully* do, *if only* people quit enabling them. The problem with this theory is that there is simply no scientific proof to it. The recovery rate is and has been 3 percent with no proof that *any* specific influences are sending that 3 percent to success. I'd like to see statistics showing what percent recovered because of either of the above or by any known method and path.

Am I advocating enabling? Absolutely not. But not because it is beneficial or detrimental to the addict. It makes no difference in their play of the heroin game. The only difference it makes is to you, the loving parent— your health, your pocketbook, your thwarted hopes and dreams. That is the reason not to do it.

4. *Setting "boundaries" with the addict is easily achievable.*

At one time, a good friend "praised" me for having a visit with my son without being tempted to give him aid of any kind. Good in theory *if* you have a heart of ice.

Imagine your loved one (or anyone) floating at sea

about to drown, and you come alongside in a boat. You didn't put this person in the water, nor will pulling them out guarantee they won't go out to sea again tomorrow. More humane to let them drown, yes? But not easy.

It tore a new hole in my heart, and I would choose rather to not see him. Remember, there are two choices: stay in the torture chamber and witness their agony *or* leave the room. *But you can't stop it.*

5. *All addicts hit rock bottom eventually.*

    Not true. Many will die by overdose, suicide, exposure, or illness before they get close to rock bottom. Many will play the heroin game board for years. Many do hit rock bottom but don't obtain sobriety. Remember the odds: 3 percent. If everyone who hit rock bottom got clean, that statistic would be a lot higher.

POPULAR MYTHS

1. Popular advice will say that addicts should be left alone, and we are doing them a disservice having contact with them. Like we don't have enough to feel guilty about. Because whether we want to admit it or not, there is a level of guilt, thinking we coulda/woulda/shoulda done *something* different in their upbringing. Guilt exists no matter the facts, even if our other children turned out fine.

    More that the unwarranted guilt trip is the *implication* that the sooner we abandon the addict, the sooner they will (A) hit rock bottom, (B) have a eureka moment, or (C) become clean and sober. Trouble is, there is no evidence to this theory.

2. If you cut off money, food, love, communication, and shelter to an addict, it will stop them from buying drugs and push them to becoming clean. The truth is that they *will* fund it from somewhere. They're not going to become clean because they ran out of resources. They may go to a rehab or shelter, but not out of a conviction to get clean, only for the survival of the moment. I've never heard of a recovered addict saying that the reason they

stopped was "no money." They may go homeless and hungry, but they'll find a way to get the drugs. *Cutting off the money supply will not* stop them from getting drugs. They'll only stop using drugs if and when they're ready. And unfortunately, there is no known surefire catalyst for that.

I suspect the "hands off" philosophy promoted by NA et al. was intended to push the addict into a corner, thus to sobriety. My theory is, forget the drug addict; enabling doesn't help or hurt the addict, but it creates great emotional and financial harm to the PoA.

3. Addicts must remove themselves from their environment, "friends," and drug connections.

    My son lived in five cities in three countries over a period of fourteen years. Everywhere he lived, he found "friends" and drug sources within weeks. One may make the assumption that drug addicts are stupid.

    Unfortunately, there is no correlation between addictive tendencies and IQ. My son has an above-average IQ and could have excelled at anything he chose to do. You can take the addict out of the environment, but the addiction goes along for the ride to the new location.

In conclusion, I know that the drug treatment facilities, doctors, and therapists have the best of intentions. The sad truth is, it's not doing much good. Once Pandora's box is opened, there's no going back for 97 percent of the addicts. I challenge any doctor or facility to show me proof that their patients have a higher cure rate than untreated addicts.

Does this mean I don't hope every day that he will be in the 3 percent? Of course I do. I'm just realistic. Statistics don't lie.

Years Eleven And Twelve

After another stint in rehab, he lives with me for several months, being watched 24/7 and staying clean. With no money and no transportation, it seems to be working, but this was no way to live. Of course, as soon as he has access to wheels and a few bucks, he is on drugs again. After another trip to rehab, he says he is ready to try life again. I have to hand it to him for hope and perseverance. I have not been able to hold onto that hope and now see the game for exactly what it is. The lessons of the warnings listed in the first chapter have been learned by watching him go around in circles but never finding the way to the finish line.

For many years, the deny ability game had allowed me to think I could still save him. That belief has now died. In its place forms an understanding of the myths and fallacies of addiction and treatment.

CATCH PHRASES OF ADDICTION TREATMENT

Enabling

It is my opinion that almost every parent enables, at least in the first months or even years of discovery of their child's addiction. Why? The obvious initial answer is that they think this will "help" in some way. There are less obvious reasons. It's human nature (even if the victim of the torture is a stranger and not your child) to want to rush in and give aid. Or there may be guilt or shame or myriad other factors influencing the behavior. The motivations are unimportant.

The fallacy is that enabling hurts the addict or delays recovery. The truth is, it does neither. For there is no cure—except for 3 percent of the victims— and no one knows why/how they are cured.

Here's a fact of human nature I find hard to grasp: the number of people willing to spew their expert advice as to how to be a PoA and how to deal with an addict. It is surprising that of all the friends, relatives, and acquaintances who have pontificated their wisdom upon me, not one was a PoA, was a trained professional in drug addiction, or had the full facts of the situation with my addict. Yet they readily heaped on the advice and criticism of my actions. How pompous.

The good news is that the PoA will come to understand that enabling serves no purpose except to drain their heart and pocketbook; then they will stop. I stopped helping my son when I finally realized that all the rehabs, all the doctors, all the Suboxone, all the enabling, was not going to cure my son, and it was sending me to financial ruin. Perhaps this information will help others to stop before they ruin themselves. Don't kick yourself if you've done it. It's a human thing to do when your child is in the torture chamber and you haven't learned that you can't break him out. I don't regret spending some time with my son over the past fourteen years. Since he most likely will not live a long life, I will treasure the few sober times I had with him on this earth.

Codependency

This behavior does exist, but labeling every PoA who enables the addict, trying to put out the fire for any period of time, as codependent is an inaccurate generalization. My son's ten-minute psychiatrist who saw him long enough to write a Suboxone prescription labeled me as codependent. She'd never met me. Some needy, lonely parents might get some gratification from "taking care" of their child, but that didn't include me, and I don't think it applies to the majority of parents who have their own busy, fulfilling lives. His addiction was a thorn in my side. All I wanted to do was run my business, enjoy my social life, and travel the world. I took no pleasure in "aiding" him, and it filled no empty nest syndrome or emotional need in me. In the beginning, I figured I could throw some money at this "ridiculous" habit and make it go away. I hadn't read the rules of the game at that time. I simply wanted his drug problem gone. The bigger question is, why is there such a need by "professionals" to want to project culpability to those surrounding the addict? Certainly, an addict is influenced by the surrounding environment, but let's not pretend we know which factors are the most influential, and let's not cast "blame" of codependency without knowing the circumstances.

It is interesting that this doctor had no problem with my paying for his treatment. The only time she saw me was at the counter paying with my credit card. If she truly believed I was doing him a disservice, why did she promote the codependency by taking my money and continuing to schedule appointments? Seems a contradiction in having the best of intentions for the patient. Money talks, BS walks!

Rehab

Although rehab was addressed in other chapters, it bears repeating that the efficacy rate of rehabs is questionable. Whether very expensive private facilities or state-run facilities, repeat visits are the norm. Is every visit a step closer to the "cure"? If that were the case, we'd have statistics on which facilities are least revisited and have the highest cure rate. None hold that distinction. There is not an "Ivy League" facility producing the majority of the 3 percent of permanently recovered addicts.

Drug Aids

Curing drug addiction with more drugs. While Suboxone cannot be used in excess to obtain the same high as heroin, it is a handy tool for the drug addict to use to avoid withdrawal when unable to obtain a heroin fix. This is the way my son used it. The intent of Suboxone is to help addicts avoid heroin, not as a supplement to it. Perhaps it is a useful aid for the 3 percent of recovered addicts. But then they are still replacing one drug with another.

Methadone has been around many years for the treatment of opiate addiction. When my son took it, it was highly controlled in dispensing clinics and very expensive. It negated the recovered addict from leaving the geographic area because doses were required to be administered by medical staff and taken on site. Had my son recovered and relied on methadone, it would have prohibited him from pursuing his profession, which required some distance travel. A small price to pay, I suppose. Whenever he took it, he appeared to me to be very high, as high as when he'd smoked heroin. This is just my layperson's observation.

Due to the cost and steps necessary to receive the dosage, he went back to street heroin.

Tough Love

There is a philosophy in the treatment of addicts that some just need tough love—a kick in the butt as it were. Go ahead if you like; heap torture on the torture. I actually hired an employee who was clean and good at her job who had been sent to Crash in San Diego, a kind of boot camp usually filled with addicts sent there by court order. I'm happy for her, although I heard recently she may be back on drugs.

I personally find it hard to believe that piling psychological torture upon the addict's self-inflicted torture is going to engender that eureka moment of a cure. I believe addicts are already mentally damaged or malfunctioning in that department. Many are products of abusive drug addict parents. So

---

how is bullying and scaring them going to cure them? Hey, whatever works, I suppose. I think it would push my son over the edge to suicide. Maybe for the best then, might be their philosophy.

Hitting Bottom

This is one of my favorite catch phrases in the drug addiction treatment world. But what does it mean? The inference I got when hearing it lectured was that somehow, when they finally bump down on the bottom of the abyss, the sky will light up with fireworks, a lightning bolt will lift them to the sky, and an epiphany of inexplicable proportions will hit them. They will see the light and be cured. So it's very, very important that we let them "hit bottom." But that it were true.

I've asked many for a definition of *bottom*—jail, hospital, homeless, overdose, near-death experience. All I hear is, it's different for everyone. Okay, then what defines it? Is it what happens to those 3 percent who are the lucky ones? Does it happen to many more than the 3 percent but doesn't lead them to sobriety? If not, what is its significance?

I'm here to say that be it jail, prison, enabling, rehab, drug supplements, tough love, or hitting bottom, *no one knows what the magic to the cure is*. Has anyone done extensive studies on the 3 percent? This is where knowledge of a cure *may* come from. And I say *may* because it is not something we know enough about yet.

I'm willing to acknowledge the fact that there has been so little progress in "curing" drug addiction in the last forty years.

Just don't appreciate the "experts" who profess to know what works and what doesn't, because if they had definitively narrowed down the possible measures that work, there would be a higher success rate.

No one knows. And maybe there is not a way to improve the odds other than convincing people not to play the game in the first place. I mean, it's not like they are compelled to play the game by being picked from a death lottery. They go into it willingly.

THE CONFLICTING THEORIES OF TREATMENT INTERVENTION VERSUS COURT ORDER VERSUS FREE WILL

Over fourteen years, I've heard various philosophies advocated. An intervention was done on my son in the second year of his use, ironically performed by the same group that later "schooled" me on not facilitating my son's entering into rehab, their philosophy changing. Their latest idea being that unless the addict goes willingly and of his own arrangement and volition, he was doomed to failure.

This "free will" philosophy seems to be the rage of the moment, yet a great many addicts are there by court order. They've broken the law, and the judge gives them the choice between jail time or rehab.

They're picking the lesser of two evils, but that does not make them a willing and hopeful participant in the rehab process.

I mention these conflicting philosophies only as a matter of interest. In my opinion, it doesn't matter how they end up in rehab. Only 3 percent are coming out recovered and staying that way for the rest of their life. Most will end up back in rehab. So what does it matter how they got there?

Years Thirteen And Fourteen

He relocates with me to a new city. This time, he is really gonna do it! He works hard at sobriety. He spends all his time doing manual labor and trying to rebuild his business, for which he renews his state certification. He leaves to attend AA and Nar-Anon meetings. Somehow, after a short while, he doesn't make it to the meetings.

In no time, his business is again failing, and all the telltale signs of drug use are there—irregular sleep pattern, pawning items, all the usual. Thanks to thirteen years of experience, I recognize the signs much more quickly than I would have in the past. I kick him out, clean his room of all the stashes and paraphernalia, and sell his car.

I suppose I'm happy for addicts when they have periods of recovery. Their "clean" times, however, often don't give them time to transition to a productive life. This is bad for the PoA in two ways: first, this is when a PoA is most vulnerable to help the "recovering" addict because he is "clean," and, second, it adds another layer to the agony when the recovery period is over and they're back on drugs.

Ever the survivor, he convinces his sister that he needs a clean break. She agrees to let him move to her home on a Caribbean island and work in a restaurant seven days per week. He would spend a year on the island to "get clean"—an island where, we were assured, opiates are completely impossible to obtain.

I visited when he had been there a year and found out in short order that he was not clean but had been using the whole time he was there. His sister had fired him and kicked him out on the street. Then the pandemic hit.

So he was on the street when the island shut down due to the COVID pandemic. Under mandatory curfew ordered by the prime minister, the island's population was under military lockdown. Anyone leaving their residence was to be arrested on sight. He moved into my hotel room to get off the street. For six weeks, we endured as everyone in the world did, only I was living side by side with an addict in withdrawal. No opiates and drugs and no hospitals or doctors. As his withdrawal went on and desperation took over, he ventured onto the streets late at night. Sneaking around in the tropical undergrowth and running through the shadows from building to building, he sought out his fix. Hunger is a big motivator, and he found what he was looking for. He traded his bike helmet, cell phone, and clothes for it. While the rest of us on the island struggled to get food and drinking water, he cared only about the drugs.

I vowed then and there that he would never be under my roof again, and he never has.

We were finally able to join a group on a chartered plane to get back to the United States, where he vowed to go into rehab. That was eight months ago. From what I hear, he's living on the streets.

What will it take to make him change? Can he change? He's been through deaths, overdoses, withdrawals, homelessness, starvation, almost freezing to death, humiliation, denigration, loneliness, filthiness, hopelessness, pain, sickness, and heartbreak. And he's no closer to stopping the game than he was the first year. I know he wants to. I know he longs for a normal life and at times tries to believe/pretend he has one.

Sometimes, when driving around the town where he grew up, and where most of the family still lives, I look for him on the corners of freeway entrance ramps. Sometimes a homeless figure standing there will catch my eye, the height and hair reminding me of my son. But it has not been him.

I don't know where he is now or what he is doing. Sometimes late at night, he texts me, "I love you, Mom." And I think he really does.

EPILOGUE

WHERE DO WE GO FROM HERE?

Our politically correct world would have us believe there is a happy ending to everything. In truth, there simply isn't. If there were a proven path to sobriety, it would be well known, as is the treatment for diabetes or infection or many other illnesses. The fact is, there is no proven or even semi-effective method of treatment. Why, if the cure rate was 3 percent in 1999, is it not 10 or 20 or 90 percent now? This has not happened.

Say whatever you want about the beliefs I've illustrated and their accuracy, but it can't be denied that addicts are not being helped.

Believe me that if love and prayers and tears and good intentions could save my son, he would be saved. Humans are made mostly of hope. We live on hope.

So what *is* the answer? How do we put the monster back in the box? Let the drug companies figure it out. They created the problem. Admittedly, it takes two to tango (the addict and the drug availability), but the number/percentage of heroin addicts since the 1980s has increased more than tenfold. For the sake of the mighty dollar, a generation has been forfeited.

It's Christmastime again. I stayed home alone on Thanksgiving, a self-imposed quarantine. The world has changed for everyone. For me, it is always a hard time of the year. I don't know where he is, but as far as I know, he is still alive.

I'm writing this from my beach house in Mexico, but I'm not really hiding out. Even though I've blocked his number, he will hear the ring if he calls and know by the different tone that I'm in Mexico.

A relative says to have him arrested if he shows up at the door. Ludicrous. First of all, the Mexican police will not arrest him for entering his mother's house, even if he's high. And if I could convince them to do so, his incarceration in a Mexican jail would be a death sentence. And for all he's put me through, I would *still* not subject him to rape, torture, and death. Call me a softie.

Where is my son now? on the streets? in rehab? in jail? I don't know.

I have been staying out of the torture chamber for now.

It's ten o'clock at night. If I hear a pounding on the door, what should I do?

NOTES AND EMAILS

2006

My experience in the last seventy-two hours dealing with his first withdrawal:

Wednesday

> Took him to urgent care at a hospital (Claremont, California). They would not admit him without a check for $10,000.
>
> Took him to his friend's to buy a "detox" pill. Gave him $30 but did not go in the house with him.

Thursday

> He went to an urgent care clinic and got two prescriptions. Gave him $200, but he came back with no receipt. Dropped him at Longs to fill the prescriptions, another $130.

Friday

> Took Xanax without my knowledge or permission. Stole the dog's painkillers.

2008

His current debts and financial reality

Credit cards	$20,000
Car loan	$26,000
Back rent	$6,000
Utilities	$500
Traffic tickets	$2,000
Attorney	$2,500

Future money needs

Rent deposit	$21,500
Doctors	$200/month

November 2008

Here's a contract his sister drew up to let him live at her house:

1. Daily drug testing
2. Sleep at home every night
3. Weekend curfew at 11:00 p.m.
4. Weekly therapy sessions
5. Weekly lunch or dinner with all the family
6. Commit to three meals a day
7. In the office at nine to five
8. Full physical to be done
9. No socializing with drug friends

Oath: If I fail to abide by these rules or to fully invest in myself and my well-being, I shall accept the terms of job loss and loss of my home and will enter myself into a rehab facility.

Every line of the contract was signed. No conditions of the contract were met.

March 6, 2009

Son,

I'm sorry, but I can't help you for the following reasons:

1. You will not be truthful with me regarding your financial situation.
2. You avoid sitting down and facing the issues. I have been chasing you for a week to sit down. It's almost comical the way you run out the door (at home and at the office), jump into bed and go to sleep, jump in the shower, fail to come home, etc. When I *do* finally pin you to the wall, you explode as though I am inconveniencing *you*. Believe me, helping you is doing *me* no favors.

I am paying your car insurance today. You have "disposed of" $500 since you cashed your paycheck two days ago. You cannot spend that way.

If you don't pay your credit cards, they will garnish your wages and you won't be able to get credit until you're in your thirties. You tell me how smart you are. Well, moving on to new credit cards is not the answer, and you know it.

I am enabling you to continue your messy, irresponsible lifestyle. As a mother, I am doing you no favors. Please move out this weekend. It is unhealthy for us to live together. I am going to counseling to deal with my relationship with you, and I suggest you go to one too.

December 1, 2009

Current prescription pill bottles in his possession:

Doctor	Drug	Date Prescribed	Amount of Pills Left	Treatment For
K/F	Alprazolam	11/06/09	10	hostility/anxiety
W	Vyvanse	11/11/09	30	ADHD
F	amphetamine	10/27/09	60	stimulant
F	*amphetamine*	11/19/09	60	?
Illegible	Vyvanse	?	0	?
Fn	amphetamine	illegible	20	stimulant

January 29, 2010

Dear Mother,

In light of my current situation, I propose to you the following solution:

1. I *need* a *job*. I have every intention of obtaining one ASAP!

   A. Résumé completed.
   B. Vehicle registered, and I'm following the payment plan with dealership.
   C. Must have living unit within Southern California.

Without having my living situation taken care of, I cannot seriously pursue another full-time job. The preceding point is the reason why I cannot afford to spend additional time on hiatus or stay in my current apartment while I await another move to an uncertain place.

If you would be willing to assist me financially with these urgent needs to get back on my feet before December, I will commit to the following:

1. Being your assistant, wage-free, plus paying portions of each of my checks until you are fully reimbursed, plus interest.
2. This includes traveling to clients and your work location as needed to complete tasks.
3. Paying out of pocket for daily drug tests.
4. Committing to any other request you or I can think of.

Sincerely,

Your son

February 12, 2010

Dear son,

Here are the conditions of the contract:

1. A budget will be made to determine length of contract to pay expenses for care.
2. Car will be inoperable until street legal.
3. You will work for me at a rate to be determined by me and to go toward car expenses. I will decide job duties.
4. You will live with me with no vehicle and travel with me at my discretion.
5. Spare time will be used to job hunt, prepare résumés, prepare life plan for end of contract, and stay healthy.
6. No drugs/pills in the house, except aspirin and antacids.
7. You will keep living quarters, clothes, and person clean at all times.
8. Termination for breach of contract at my discretion.

July 19, 2010

Mom, you continue to give more to your daughter, and yet you won't even talk to be. You could care less if I was dead. My best friend's mom helps me more than you. She believes family should stick together. You show your boyfriend more respect and love than your own son.

Son, you may think of the rehab place as a kind of jail, but it's not. They will not only provide a warm, dry bed but also food, which I am sure you are not getting. They will also help you to get a copy of the paperwork for your court date and provide support and counseling, because everything you have been through in the last couple of years, they already know about. They also know that drug abuse can be caused by other problems, such as depression, broken families, etc. This could be the doorway to finding a path out and other entities which can provide ongoing support so you don't relapse like your friend has.

October 2010

Son,

Here's a little true/false questionnaire for you:

1. I spend an inordinate amount of time talking about drugs, their uses, effects, side effects and have an unusual interest in the drugs in others' medicine chests.
2. I regularly attend counseling therapy or NA meeting.
3. I have admitted to and planned recompense for those I have hurt financially and emotionally.
4. I have a game plan to avoid drugs and relapse in the future.
5. I am following the steps of the game plans/goals set with my adviser when I went through withdrawal.

December 2010

Son,

Here are the options:

Option 1: Mom acting as detox/rehab caregiver. Won't work because

1. I have limited knowledge and *no* experience in substance abuse care.
2. Even if I did have a degree in this, treating your own son is not appropriate.
3. I do not have time or skills to frisk daily, check whereabouts 24/7, search house and car constantly, hide money, and do constant cleanup of messes left.

Option 2: Professional care by outside party. Our limited research in this regard reveals that

1. Your insurance is not adequate for coverage.
2. Private rehabs are about $1,000/day.
3. State rehabs are more like an education in additional recreational substances and how to obtain them.

Option 3: You on your own. Can't see it working because

1. You're financially insolvent.
2. You're likely depressed and suicidal.
3. You don't have the strength to get clean *with* love and help, so you may do worse without it.

January 21, 2011

Son,

How well are you using your time? Are you keeping regular hours? When is your next NA meeting? I'd like to see your financial status chart and your bill payment schedule.

Have you applied for disability?

We need to discuss your progress and improvement. You need to pay your outstanding ticket then close your bank account.

2013

Son,

Wednesday you left to make a site visit for your job. You came back two hours later, sweating and wired. You spent the day chatting and picking at sores. I know you are using again.

Friday you left again to make another site visit. Came back three hours later, sweating and wired. Hyper the rest of the day and with an aggressive mood. You insist you are not using, but I know you are lying.

Saturday you said you had completed your online semester, but you didn't.

You're angry that the doctor wouldn't refill your amphetamine prescription five days early. Your room is a disgusting junk pile.

Sunday you found every hiding place I used for your prescribed medication and continued to self-medicate. Childish behavior and aggression continue.

Time for you to get out again. You're always out of money, covered in sores, losing weight, and using inhalers. Full-on addict again.

Oh, and I discovered your unpaid traffic ticket, drug remnants in the house, everything you own filthy, and a pawn slip for your computer. And you're hanging out with again.

I cannot babysit you and try to protect you from yourself. Good luck.

March 12, 2014

Son,

It is best you move to Utah and live with your dad. Your dad will have to decide whether to help you make insurance payments or what he will expect from you if you live with him.

May 2016

Son,

So here you are again in San Diego. You have not been to the dentist, completed the twelve-step program, or completed your real estate license renewal. In addition, you have again "lost" your driver's license, passport, and your smartphone and clipboard and two briefcases.

You need to get documents replaced and get into rehab. I cannot help you.

March 24, 2017

Son,

It is obvious you are back on drugs again because

    –   You are not taking your Suboxone.

- You have money and transportation to buy the drugs.
- You are befriending your druggy friends again.
- Your sleep patterns are erratic.
- You are not eating much.
- Sores are again appearing on your neck.
- You're sneaking into my house looking for money.
- Not keeping commitments.
- Erratic work hours.
- Not going to NA meetings.
- Moody and hyper.

No need for a drug test. Time for you to go to rehab. Again.

2018

Son,

Now that I am moving, I want to address some concerns. You've done a great job helping me with repair and sale of the house.

It's the punch list items I'm concerned with. I saw you feverishly researching your car online and tinkering with it. Your priorities should be researching better health insurance, finding a local doctor, getting a lower car interest rate, etc. Also, working harder on your business.

These things come first, and it would save $500–$1,000 per month. You know how broke you are, and I can't let you take advantage of my kindness and generosity.

I know you are a recovering drug addict, but this behavior cannot go on.

March 2020

Dear Mom,

You asked me why I can't seem to get off drugs.

Self-guilt causes anxiety, which reinforces inclination to continue to relapse, to alleviate anxiety. Boredom and lack of positive feelings (which should be naturally produced) are my key reasons to use. Overwhelming compulsion to continue the activity that gives me pleasure indicates my addictive nature.

April 2020

(This is the last letter I wrote to my son.)

Son,

This is an end to the hurt you have done to your own family

I really think you want to be an addict. Only now you have no money, so you will have to be a criminal to do it.

Take the situation of what is going on in the world now as a moment of contemplation, and maybe you can turn your life around.

I've always wished I could understand the hunger. From a parent's point of view, all it does is make your behavior and mood weird. You said it doesn't make you feel good anymore, just stops the depression and withdrawal.

Fourteen years of all this with you. In your twenties, I tried to keep you from getting a criminal record so you would not ruin the rest of your life. In your thirties, I realized your chance to make something of your life had already negated a positive future.

In fourteen years, you have ruined your health, your résumé, your reputation; scarred your body; and ruined your teeth. You've spent every cent you ever earned and thousands of my hard-earned dollars. You've alienated everyone who loves you, and you turned into a sneak and a liar.

What have you gained? Absolutely nothing but a knowledge of a seedy underworld and how to lie and cheat in it. You sacrificed having a long life with a family.

And you still believe you can be a functioning addict, have an income, a career while using?

In fourteen years, you have been unable to kick the habit. I pride myself in being very smart, but in fourteen years, I have not been able to figure out any way to help you, not that it's my problem to solve.

In fourteen years, nothing has motivated you to quit—not your friend's overdose death, not your father's death, not seeing the pain you've caused the rest of your family. Nothing has given you a "eureka" moment.

In fourteen years, you have lived in two states and three countries. The longest you have been clean is four months. As soon as you become familiar with a new venue, you find your way to the drugs. Every time you are comfortable with your friends and loved ones, you use their love for you against them and begin to sneak, lie, and steal from them. I wish you could see how much your disease and addiction have hurt the people who love you.

So what's the answer? I don't have one, and I'm convinced I never will.

Your sister and I have continued to help, and through it all, we've been told we are "controlling" you.

Well, it's over. You will either get clean or die. Getting on your feet by yourself will be the hardest thing you could ever do, but it can be done. Maybe at *some time* you'll look back and be amazed at how far you've come. I hope that happens, but I can no longer be around to watch and wait.

INDEX

Q

quacks, 14, 56

R

rationalization technique, 49
recovery, 40, 51, 54–55, 57, 59–60, 72
  debunking fallacies of, 59
rehab process, 70
rehab return rate, 48
rehabs, 24, 41, 48, 53–54, 60, 63, 66–67, 70, 80
  county, 57
  court-ordered, 23
  private, 82
  state, 82
  state-run, 53
relapse, 44, 81, 84
relationships, 20, 31–32, 39, 50, 79

S

San Diego, 47–48, 53–54, 68, 83
society, 10–11, 13, 20–21, 26–27, 37, 39, 56–57, 60
Suboxone, 57–58, 67–68, 83
support, 30, 37, 42, 81
survival techniques, 31
survivor, 72

T

therapists, 9, 11, 40, 55, 64
torture chamber, 42, 47, 56, 62–63, 67, 76
treatment, 10–11, 13, 15, 30–31, 40, 48–49, 53–60, 64, 66–69, 75, 79
  drug, 11, 58–59, 64
  long-term, 56
treatment centers, 11, 15, 59

treatment intervention, conflicting theories of, 69
tricks of the trade, 38

W

withdrawal, 18, 26, 58, 68, 72, 77, 81, 85

X

Xanax, 57, 77

CPSIA information can be obtained
at www.ICGtesting.com
Printed in the USA
LVHW012353290321
682892LV00012B/790

9 781664 162334